DRUMSET CONTROL
DYNAMIC EXERCISES FOR INCREASED FACILITY ON THE DRUMSET

By Ron Spagnardi

Design And Layout By Joe King

Published By
Modern Drummer Publications, Inc.
12 Old Bridge Road
Cedar Grove, NJ 07009, USA

CONTENTS

INTRODUCTION

The ability to move swiftly around the drumset with speed, control, and accuracy is an extremely important asset for today's drummer. *Drumset Control* offers a progressive series of exercises designed to help you attain a substantial level of technical facility on the kit.

The format for *Drumset Control* is simple and direct. The book begins with basic triplet patterns around the drums, followed by 16th notes, 16th-note triplets, and 32nd notes. Each section is further divided into groupings, beginning with *one* grouping of each note value and progressing to *four* consecutive groupings.

A selection of sticking patterns is applied, and these offer a wealth of possibilities for moving around the drumkit. Examples of two-bar patterns and fill-ins are also included.

To Achieve The Best Results...
1) Be sure to play each exercise precisely as written, with careful focus on stickings.
2) Make certain you're comfortable with the stickings that appear above each series of patterns before attempting to play the exercises.
3) Practice each pattern slowly at first, until movement from drum to drum is smooth and flowing.
4) Repeat each exercise at least *ten times* before moving on. Do not move to the next pattern until the previous one has been mastered.
5) Make an effort to get your eyes *out of the book* as soon as possible. Focus on the movement around the drums and the *feel* of each pattern.
6) Eventually work all exercises up to *top speed*. Use a metronome or drum machine to gauge your progress.
7) Play the bass drum on 1, 2, 3, and 4 of every measure.
8) Play the hi-hat: a) on 2 and 4, b) using quarter notes, c) using 8th notes.
9) Be sure to master the one-bar exercises before attempting the two-bar patterns and fill-ins.

For an additional challenge...
10) Play through an entire page without stopping, working each pattern four times, then twice, then once. Start slowly and increase the tempo as your facility improves.
11) Certain patterns in this book lend themselves well to bass drum development. Try the following: a) substitute the bass drum for all snare drum notes, b) substitute the bass drum for all tom-tom notes. Maintain the specified stickings when using bass drum substitutions.

The following abbreviations are used throughout:
SD = Snare Drum
RRT = Right Rack Tom
LRT = Left Rack Tom
LTT = Large Tom Tom
HH = Hi-Hat
RC = Ride Cymbal
BD = Bass Drum

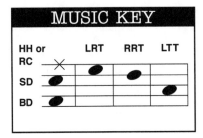

PART 1: TRIPLETS
One Group Of Triplets

Sticking: RLR-L

Sticking: LRL-R

Two Groups Of Triplets

Sticking: RLR-LRL-R

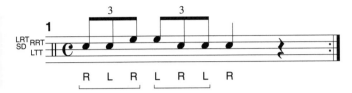

Sticking: LRL-RLR-L

Sticking: RRL-LRR-L

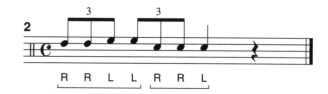

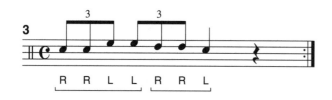

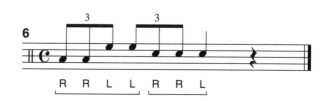

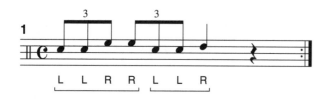

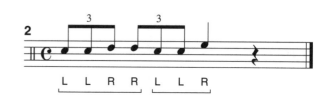

Sticking: LLR-RLL-R

Sticking: RLR-RLR-L

1

R L R R L R L

2

R L R R L R L

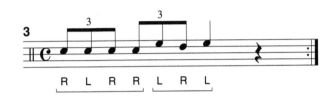

3

R L R R L R L

4

R L R R L R L

5

R L R R L R L

6

R L R R L R L

Sticking: RRL-RLR-L

1

R R L R L R L

2

R R L R L R L

3

R R L R L R L

4

R R L R L R L

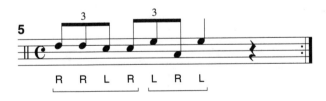

5

R R L R L R L

6

R R L R L R L

Sticking: RRL-RRL-R

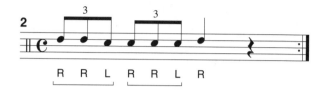

Sticking: LLR-LLR-L

Three Groups Of Triplets

Sticking: RLR-LRL-RLR-L

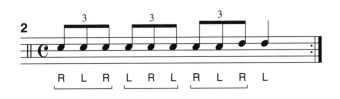

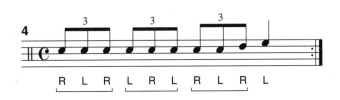

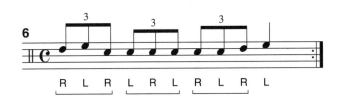

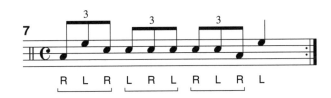

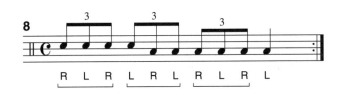

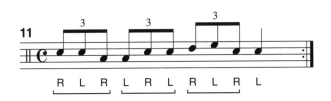

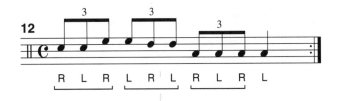

Sticking: RRL-LRR-LLR-L

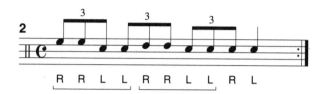

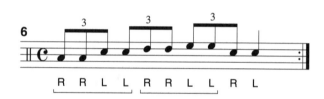

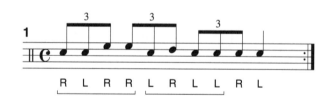

Sticking: RLR-RLR-LLR-L

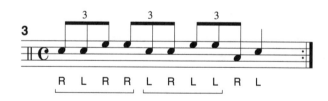

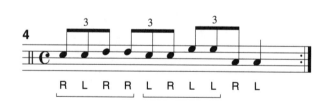

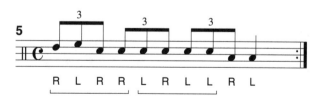

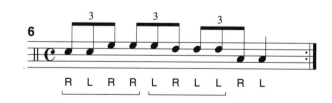

10

Sticking: RLL-RLL-RLL-R

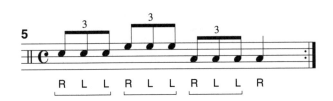

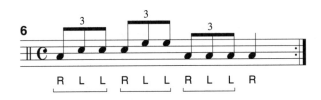

Sticking: RRL-RRL-RRL-R

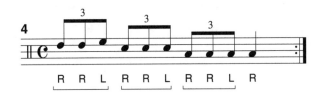

Four Groups Of Triplets

Sticking: RLR-LRL-RLR-LRL

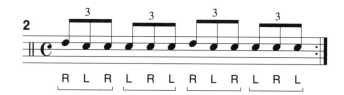

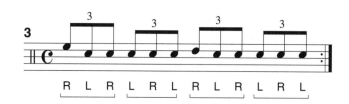

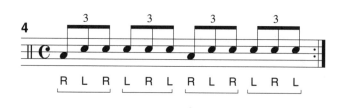

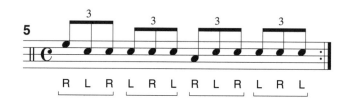

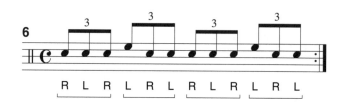

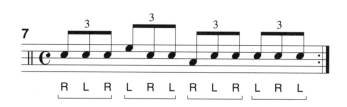

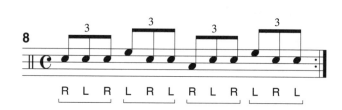

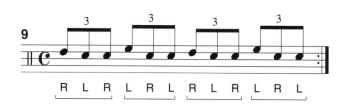

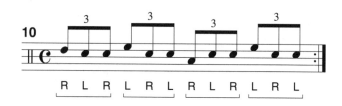

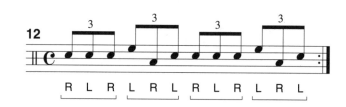

12

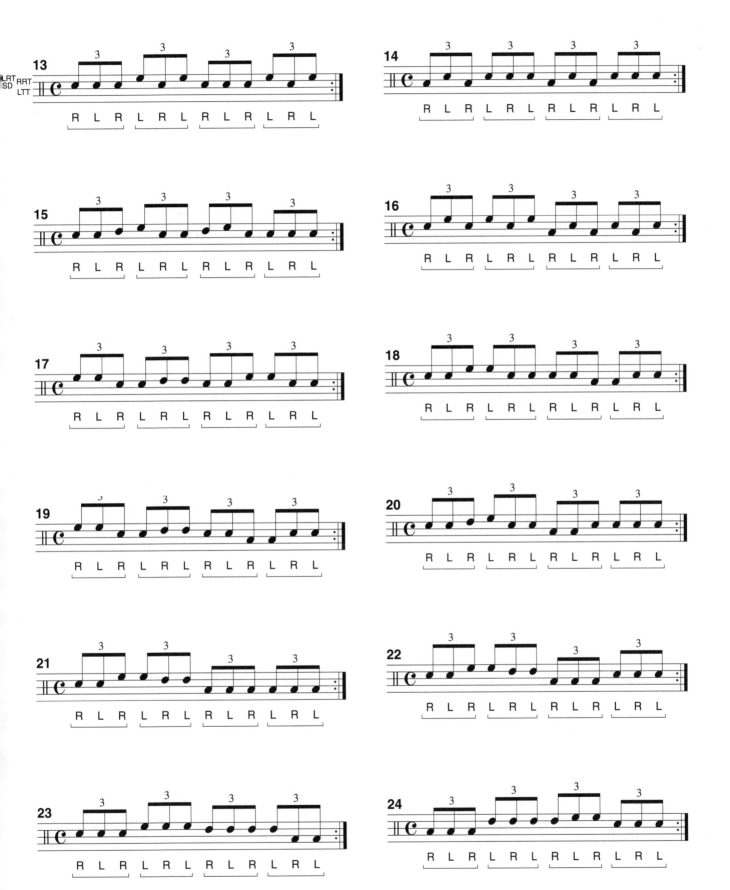

Sticking: RRL-LRR-LLR-RLL

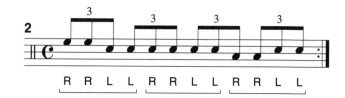

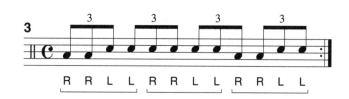

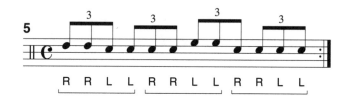

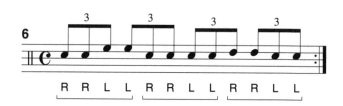

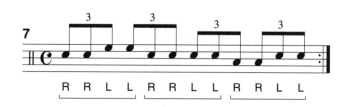

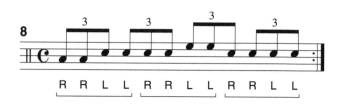

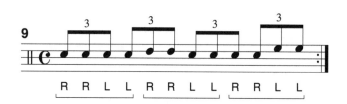

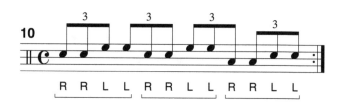

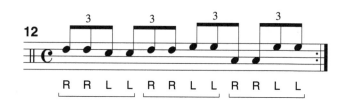

14

Sticking: RLL-RLL-RLL-RLL

1

R L L R L L R L L R L L

2
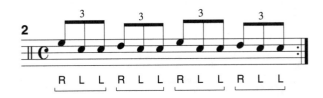
R L L R L L R L L R L L

3

R L L R L L R L L R L L

4

R L L R L L R L L R L L

5
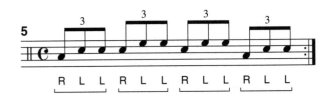
R L L R L L R L L R L L

6
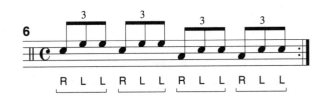
R L L R L L R L L R L L

Sticking: RRL-RRL-RRL-RRL

1
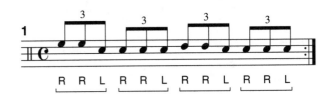
R R L R R L R R L R R L

2

R R L R R L R R L R R L

3
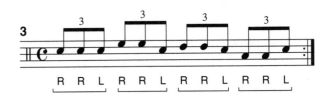
R R L R R L R R L R R L

4

R R L R R L R R L R R L

5
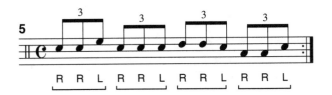
R R L R R L R R L R R L

6

R R L R R L R R L R R L

Two-Bar Patterns

Practice these patterns slowly at first and focus on accuracy. Note that the sticking changes from one bar to the next in every example. Repeat each exercise until the two bars flow smoothly together. Increase the tempo gradually.

Triplet Fills

Each of the one-bar fills below are preceded by three bars of the jazz time beat. Be sure to strive for a smooth and even time flow as you move from the time pattern into and out of the fill bar. Also practice the exercises at varied tempos and dynamics. (* Note that the final cymbal note on the "ah" of 4 should be omitted during the third repeat of the time pattern.)

PART 2: 16TH NOTES
One Group Of 16th Notes

Sticking: RLRL-R

Sticking: RRLL-R

ticking: RRLL-R-LLRR-L

1

R R L L R   L L R R L

2

R R L L R   L L R R L

3

R R L L R   L L R R L

4

R R L L R   L L R R L

5

R R L L R   L L R R L

6

R R L L R   L L R R L

Sticking: RLRR-L LRLL-R

1

R L R R L   L R L L R

2

R L R R L   L R L L R

3

R L R R L   L R L L R

4

R L R R L   L R L L R

5

R L R R L   L R L L R

6

R L R R L   L R L L R

Two Groups Of 16th Notes

Sticking: RLRL-RLRL-R

R L R L R L R L R

R L R L R L R L R

R L R L R L R L R

R L R L R L R L R

R L R L R L R L R

R L R L R L R L R

R L R L R L R L R

R L R L R L R L R

R L R L R L R L R

R L R L R L R L R

R L R L R L R L R

R L R L R L R L R

ticking: RRLL-RRLL-R

1

2

3

4

5

6

7

8

9

10

11

12

Sticking: RLRR-LRLL-R

1

R L R R L R L L R

2

R L R R L R L L R

3

R L R R L R L L R

4

R L R R L R L L R

5

R L R R L R L L R

6

R L R R L R L L R

7
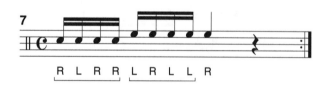
R L R R L R L L R

8

R L R R L R L L R

9

R L R R L R L L R

10

R L R R L R L L R

11

R L R R L R L L R

12

R L R R L R L L R

22

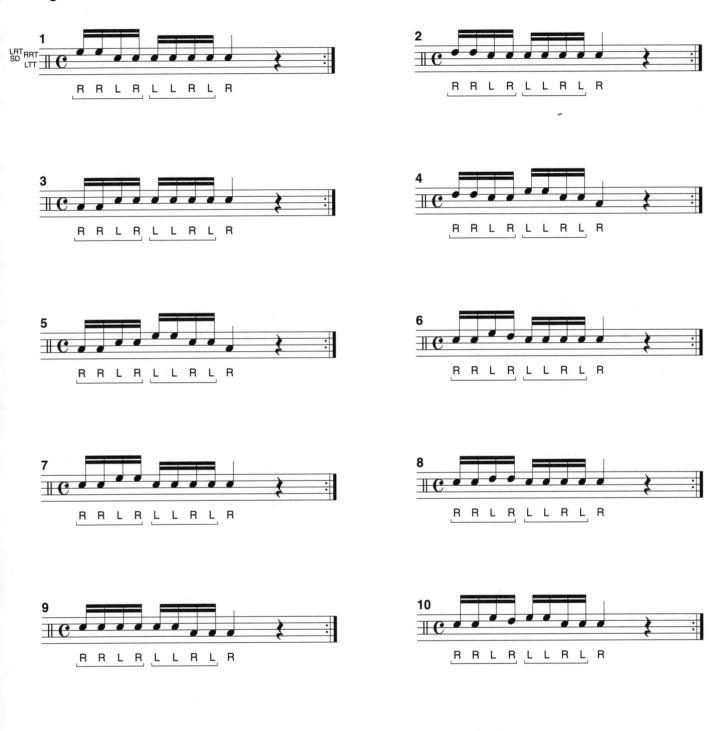

Three Groups Of 16th Notes

Sticking: RLRL-RLRL-RLRL-R

1

R L R L R L R L R L R L R

2

R L R L R L R L R L R L R

3

R L R L R L R L R L R L R

4

R L R L R L R L R L R L R

5

R L R L R L R L R L R L R

6

R L R L R L R L R L R L R

7

R L R L R L R L R L R L R

8

R L R L R L R L R L R L R

9

R L R L R L R L R L R L R

10

R L R L R L R L R L R L R

11

R L R L R L R L R L R L R

12

R L R L R L R L R L R L R

24

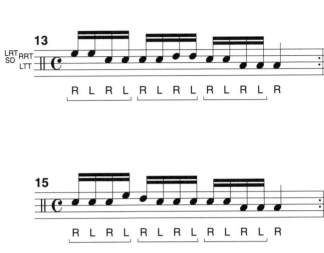

13
RLRL RLRL RLRL R

14
RLRL RLRL RLRL R

15
RLRL RLRL RLRL R

16
RLRL RLRL RLRL R

17
RLRL RLRL RLRL R

18
RLRL RLRL RLRL R

19
RLRL RLRL RLRL R

20
RLRL RLRL RLRL R

21
RLRL RLRL RLRL R

22
RLRL RLRL RLRL R

23
RLRL RLRL RLRL R

24
RLRL RLRL RLRL R

Sticking: RRLL-RRLL-RRLL-R

1

LRT RRT
SD LTT

R R L L R R L L R R L L R

2

R R L L R R L L R R L L R

3

R R L L R R L L R R L L R

4

R R L L R R L L R R L L R

5

R R L L R R L L R R L L R

6

R R L L R R L L R R L L R

7

R R L L R R L L R R L L R

8

R R L L R R L L R R L L R

9

R R L L R R L L R R L L R

10

R R L L R R L L R R L L R

11

R R L L R R L L R R L L R

12

R R L L R R L L R R L L R

26

Sticking: RLRR-LRLL-RLRR-L

1

R L R R L R L L R L R R L

2

R L R R L R L L R L R R L

3

R L R R L R L L R L R R L

4

R L R R L R L L R L R R L

5

R L R R L R L L R L R R L

6

R L R R L R L L R L R R L

7

R L R R L R L L R L R R L

8

R L R R L R L L R L R R L

9

R L R R L R L L R L R R L

10

R L R R L R L L R L R R L

11

R L R R L R L L R L R R L

12

R L R R L R L L R L R R L

Sticking: RRLR-LLRL-RRLR-L

R R L R L L R L R R L R L

R R L R L L R L R R L R L

R R L R L L R L R R L R L

R R L R L L R L R R L R L

R R L R L L R L R R L R L

R R L R L L R L R R L R L

R R L R L L R L R R L R L

R R L R L L R L R R L R L

R R L R L L R L R R L R L

R R L R L L R L R R L R L

R R L R L L R L R R L R L

R R L R L L R L R R L R L

28

Four Groups Of 16th Notes

Sticking: RLRL-RLRL-RLRL-RLRL

1
LRT RRT
SD LTT

R L R L R L R L R L R L R L R L

2

R L R L R L R L R L R L R L R L

3

R L R L R L R L R L R L R L R L

4

R L R L R L R L R L R L R L R L

5

R L R L R L R L R L R L R L R L

6

R L R L R L R L R L R L R L R L

7

R L R L R L R L R L R L R L R L

8

R L R L R L R L R L R L R L R L

9

R L R L R L R L R L R L R L R L

10

R L R L R L R L R L R L R L R L

11

R L R L R L R L R L R L R L R L

12

R L R L R L R L R L R L R L R L

13

R L R L R L R L R L R L R L R L

14

R L R L R L R L R L R L R L R L

15

R L R L R L R L R L R L R L R L

16

R L R L R L R L R L R L R L R L

17

R L R L R L R L R L R L R L R L

18

R L R L R L R L R L R L R L R L

19

R L R L R L R L R L R L R L R L

20

R L R L R L R L R L R L R L R L

21

R L R L R L R L R L R L R L R L

22

R L R L R L R L R L R L R L R L

23

R L R L R L R L R L R L R L R L

24

R L R L R L R L R L R L R L R L

Sticking: RRLL-RRLL-RRLL-RRLL

1

LRT RRT
SD
LTT

R R L L R R L L R R L L R R L L

2

R R L L R R L L R R L L R R L L

3

R R L L R R L L R R L L R R L L

4

R R L L R R L L R R L L R R L L

5

R R L L R R L L R R L L R R L L

6

R R L L R R L L R R L L R R L L

7

R R L L R R L L R R L L R R L L

8

R R L L R R L L R R L L R R L L

9

R R L L R R L L R R L L R R L L

10

R R L L R R L L R R L L R R L L

11

R R L L R R L L R R L L R R L L

12

R R L L R R L L R R L L R R L L

Sticking: RLRR-LRLL-RLRR-LRLL

1

LRT RRT
SD LTT

R L R R L R L L R L R R L R L L

2

R L R R L R L L R L R R L R L L

3

R L R R L R L L R L R R L R L L

4

R L R R L R L L R L R R L R L L

5

R L R R L R L L R L R R L R L L

6

R L R R L R L L R L R R L R L L

7

R L R R L R L L R L R R L R L L

8

R L R R L R L L R L R R L R L L

9

R L R R L R L L R L R R L R L L

10

R L R R L R L L R L R R L R L L

11

R L R R L R L L R L R R L R L L

12

R L R R L R L L R L R R L R L L

1

R R L R L L R L R R L R L L R L

2

R R L R L L R L R R L R L L R L

3

R R L R L L R L R R L R L L R L

4

R R L R L L R L R R L R L L R L

5

R R L R L L R L R R L R L L R L

6

R R L R L L R L R R L R L L R L

7

R R L R L L R L R R L R L L R L

8

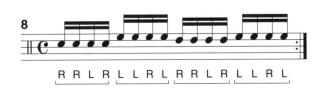

R R L R L L R L R R L R L L R L

9

R R L R L L R L R R L R L L R L

10

R R L R L L R L R R L R L L R L

11

R R L R L L R L R R L R L L R L

12

R R L R L L R L R R L R L L R L

Two-Bar Patterns

Practice these patterns slowly at first and focus on accuracy. Note that the sticking changes from one bar to the next in every example. Repeat each exercise until the two bars flow smoothly together. Increase the tempo gradually.

16th-Note Fills

Each of the one-bar fills below are preceded by three bars of an 8th-note rock pattern. Here again, focus on achieving a smooth, even time flow as you move from the rock beat into and out of the fill bar. Also practice the exercises at varied tempos and dynamics.

PART 3: 16TH-NOTE TRIPLETS
One Group Of 16th-Note Triplets

Sticking: RLRLRL-R

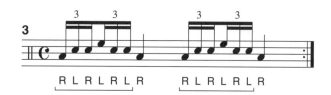

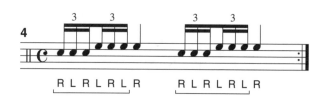

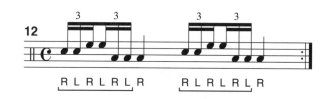

36

1

L R L R L R L   L R L R L R L

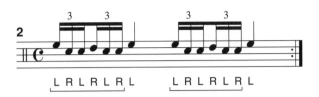

2

L R L R L R L   L R L R L R L

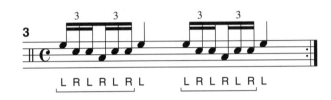

3

L R L R L R L   L R L R L R L

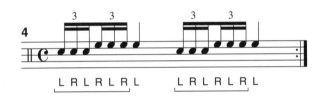

4

L R L R L R L   L R L R L R L

5

L R L R L R L   L R L R L R L

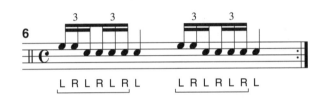

6

L R L R L R L   L R L R L R L

7

L R L R L R L   L R L R L R L

8

L R L R L R L   L R L R L R L

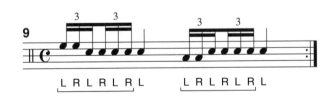

9

L R L R L R L   L R L R L R L

10

L R L R L R L   L R L R L R L

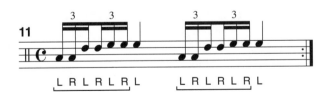

11

L R L R L R L   L R L R L R L

12

L R L R L R L   L R L R L R L

Sticking: RRLLRR-L

1
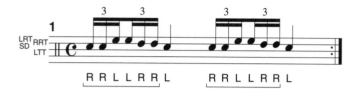

2

3

4

5
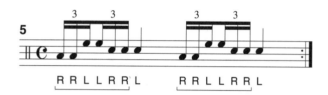

6
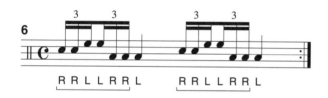

Sticking: RLRRLL-R

1

2

3

4

5

6

Two Groups Of 16th-Note Triplets

Sticking: RLRLRL-RLRLRL-R

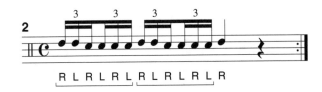

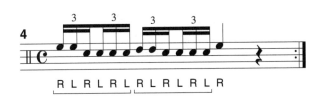

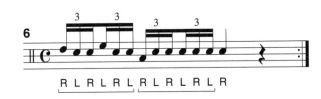

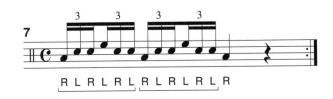

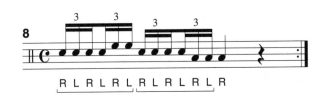

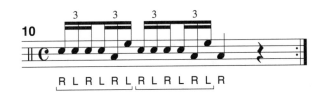

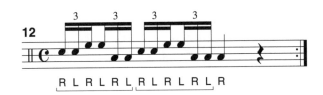

Sticking: RRLLRR-LLRRLL-R

1
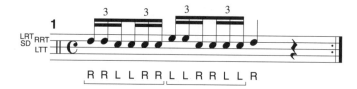

2
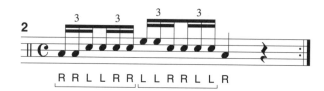

3
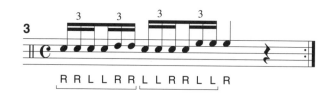

4
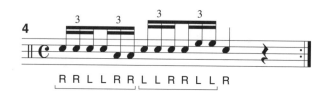

5
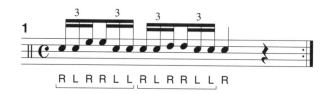

6
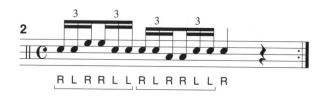

Sticking: RLRRLL-RLRRLL-R

1

2

3
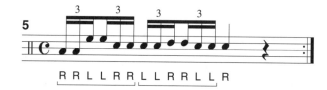

4
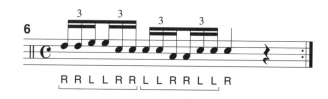

5

6
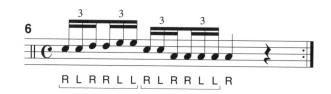

Sticking: RRLLRL-RRLLRL-R

1

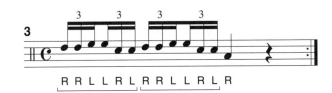

2

3

4

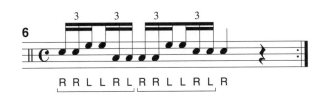

5

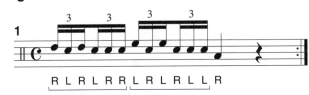

6

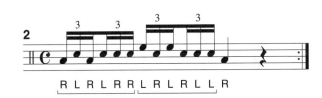

Sticking: RLRLRR-LRLRLL-R

1

2

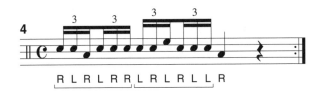

3

4

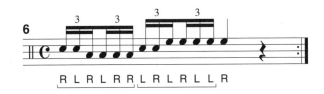

5

6

Sticking: RRLRRL-RRLRRL-R

1
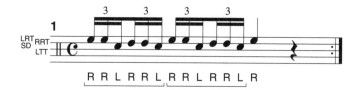

RRLRRLRRLRRLR

2

RRLRRLRRLRRLR

3

RRLRRLRRLRRLR

4

RRLRRLRRLRRLR

5

RRLRRLRRLRRLR

6

RRLRRLRRLRRLR

Sticking: LLRLLR-LLRLLR-L

1
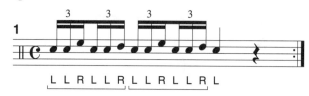

LLRLLRLLRLLRL

2

LLRLLRLLRLLRL

3

LLRLLRLLRLLRL

4

LLRLLRLLRLLRL

5

LLRLLRLLRLLRL

6
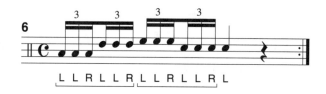

LLRLLRLLRLLRL

42

Three Groups Of 16th-Note Triplets

Sticking: RLRLRL-RLRLRL-RLRLRL-R

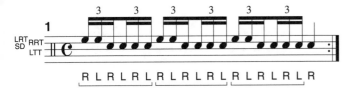

1

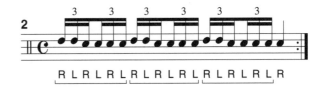

2

3

4

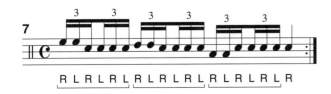

5

6

7

8

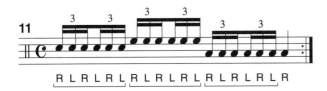

9

10

11

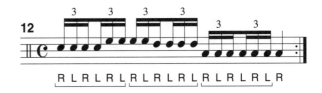

12

Sticking: RRLLRR-LLRRLL-RRLLRR-L

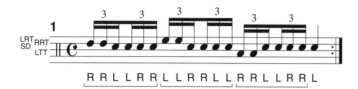

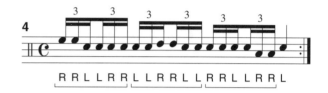

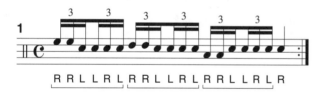

Sticking: RRLLRL-RRLLRL-RRLLRL-R

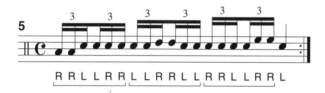

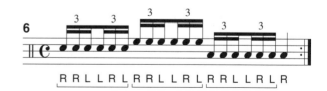

Sticking: **RLRLRR-LRLRLL-RLRLRR-L**

1

R L R L R R L R L R L L R L R L R R L

2

R L R L R R L R L R L L R L R L R R L

3

R L R L R R L R L R L L R L R L R R L

4
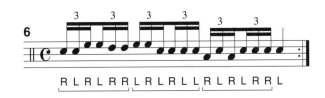

R L R L R R L R L R L L R L R L R R L

5

R L R L R R L R L R L L R L R L R R L

6

R L R L R R L R L R L L R L R L R R L

Sticking: **RRLRRL-RRLRRL-RRLRRL-R**

1

R R L R R L R R L R R L R R L R R L R

2

R R L R R L R R L R R L R R L R R L R

3

R R L R R L R R L R R L R R L R R L R

4

R R L R R L R R L R R L R R L R R L R

5

R R L R R L R R L R R L R R L R R L R

6

R R L R R L R R L R R L R R L R R L R

Four Groups Of 16th-Note Triplets

Sticking: RLRLRL-RLRLRL-RLRLRL-RLRLRL

1

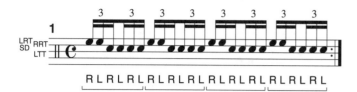

RLRLRLRLRLRLRLRLRLRLRLRL

2

RLRLRLRLRLRLRLRLRLRLRLRL

3

RLRLRLRLRLRLRLRLRLRLRLRL

4

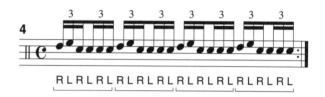

RLRLRLRLRLRLRLRLRLRLRLRL

5

RLRLRLRLRLRLRLRLRLRLRLRL

6

RLRLRLRLRLRLRLRLRLRLRLRL

7

RLRLRLRLRLRLRLRLRLRLRLRL

8

RLRLRLRLRLRLRLRLRLRLRLRL

9

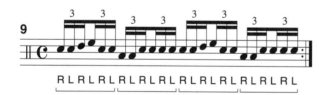

RLRLRLRLRLRLRLRLRLRLRLRL

10

RLRLRLRLRLRLRLRLRLRLRLRL

11

RLRLRLRLRLRLRLRLRLRLRLRL

12

RLRLRLRLRLRLRLRLRLRLRLRL

46

Sticking: **RRLLRR-LLRRLL-RRLLRR-LLRRLL**

1

2

3

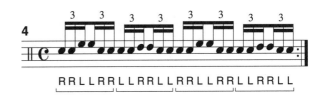

4

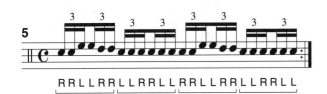

5

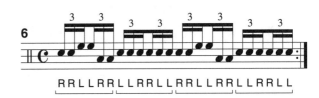

6

7

8

9

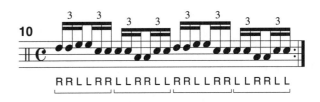

10

11

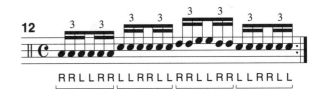

12

Sticking: RRLLRL-RRLLRL-RRLLRL-RRLLRL

1

R R L L R L R R L L R L R R L L R L R R L L R L

2

R R L L R L R R L L R L R R L L R L R R L L R L

3
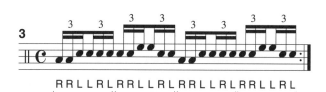
R R L L R L R R L L R L R R L L R L R R L L R L

4

R R L L R L R R L L R L R R L L R L R R L L R L

5

R R L L R L R R L L R L R R L L R L R R L L R L

6

R R L L R L R R L L R L R R L L R L R R L L R L

Sticking: RLRLRR-LRLRLL-RLRLRR-LRLRLL

1
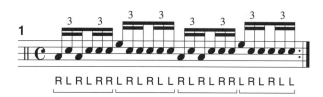
R L R L R R L R L R L L R L R L R R L R L R L L

2

R L R L R R L R L R L L R L R L R R L R L R L L

3

R L R L R R L R L R L L R L R L R R L R L R L L

4

R L R L R R L R L R L L R L R L R R L R L R L L

5

R L R L R R L R L R L L R L R L R R L R L R L L

6

R L R L R R L R L R L L R L R L R R L R L R L L

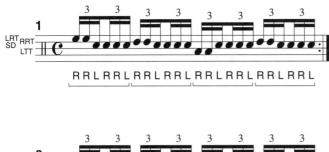

1 RRLRRLRRLRRLRRLRRLRRLRRL

 **2** RRLRRLRRLRRLRRLRRLRRLRRL

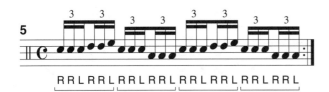 **3** RRLRRLRRLRRLRRLRRLRRLRRL

 **4** RRLRRLRRLRRLRRLRRLRRLRRL

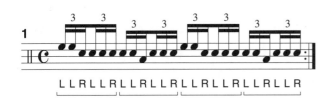 **5** RRLRRLRRLRRLRRLRRLRRLRRL

 **6** RRLRRLRRLRRLRRLRRLRRLRRL

 **1** LLRLLRLLRLLRLLRLLRLLRLLR

 **2** LLRLLRLLRLLRLLRLLRLLRLLR

 **3** LLRLLRLLRLLRLLRLLRLLRLLR

 **4** LLRLLRLLRLLRLLRLLRLLRLLR

5 LLRLLRLLRLLRLLRLLRLLRLLR

 **6** LLRLLRLLRLLRLLRLLRLLRLLR

49

Two-Bar Patterns

Here again, watch the sticking change between the first and second bars of the following patterns. Practice the exercises slowly at first and strive for a smooth flow from one bar to the next.

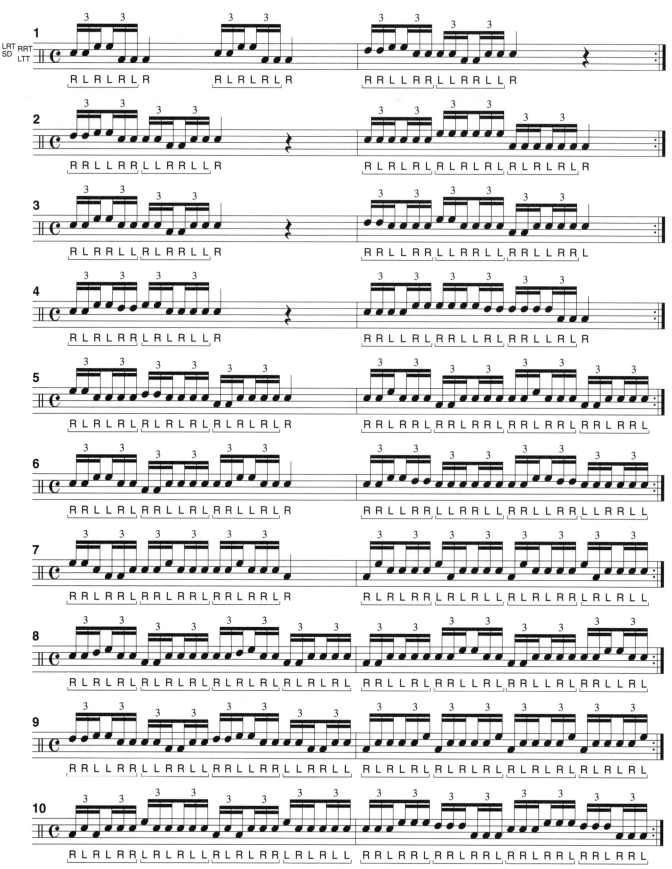

16th-Note-Triplet Fills

Each of the 16th-note-triplet fills that follow are preceded by three bars of a half-time shuffle feel. Practice these patterns at medium tempo. Be sure the time feel remains steady and even through the 16th-note-triplet fill bar.

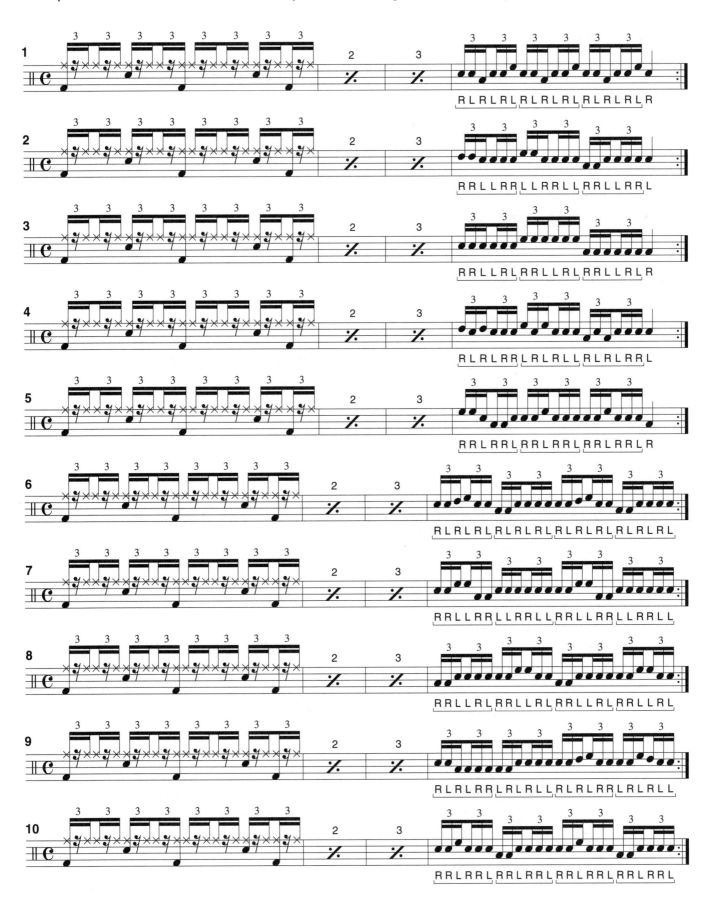

PART 4: 32ND NOTES
One Group Of 32nd Notes

Sticking: RLRLRLRL-R RLRLRLRL-R

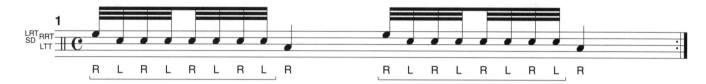

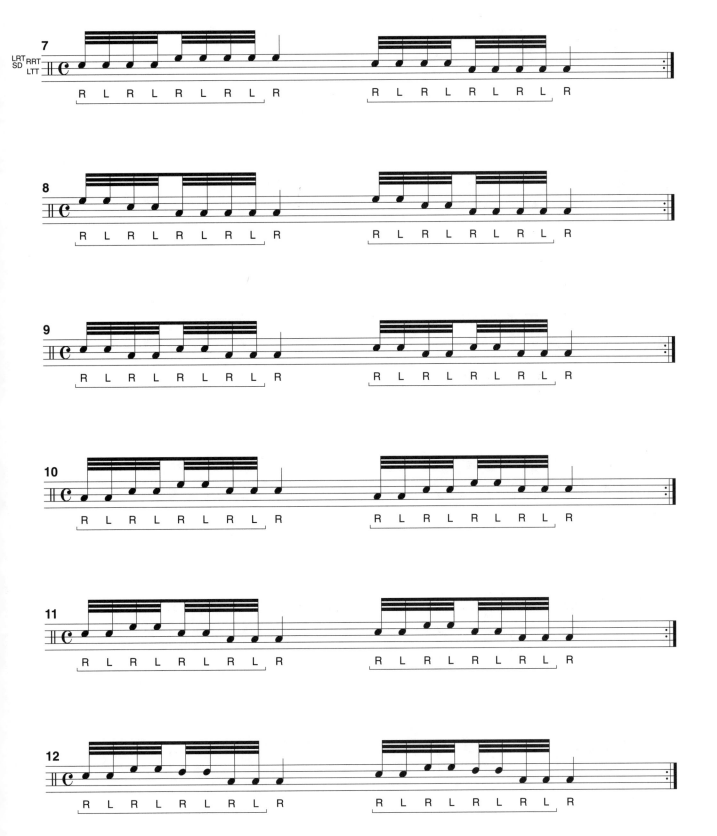

Sticking: RRLLRRLL-R RRLLRRLL-R

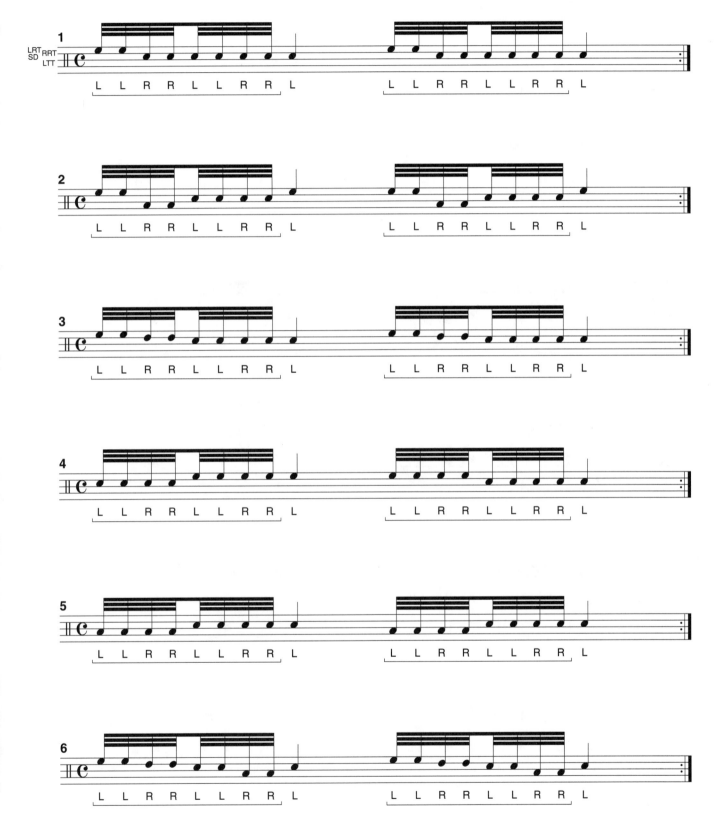

Sticking: RLRRLRLL-R RLRRLRLL-R

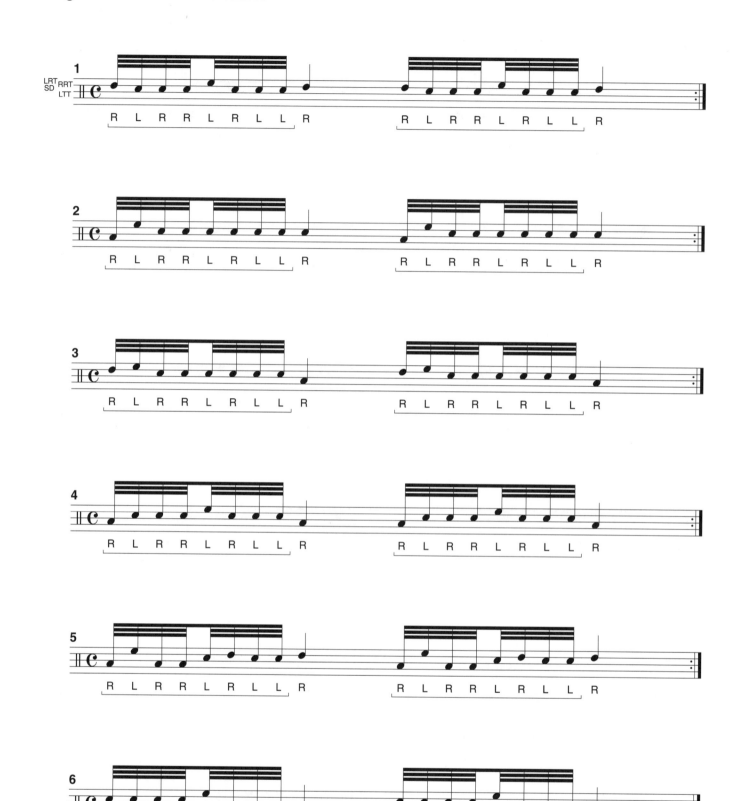

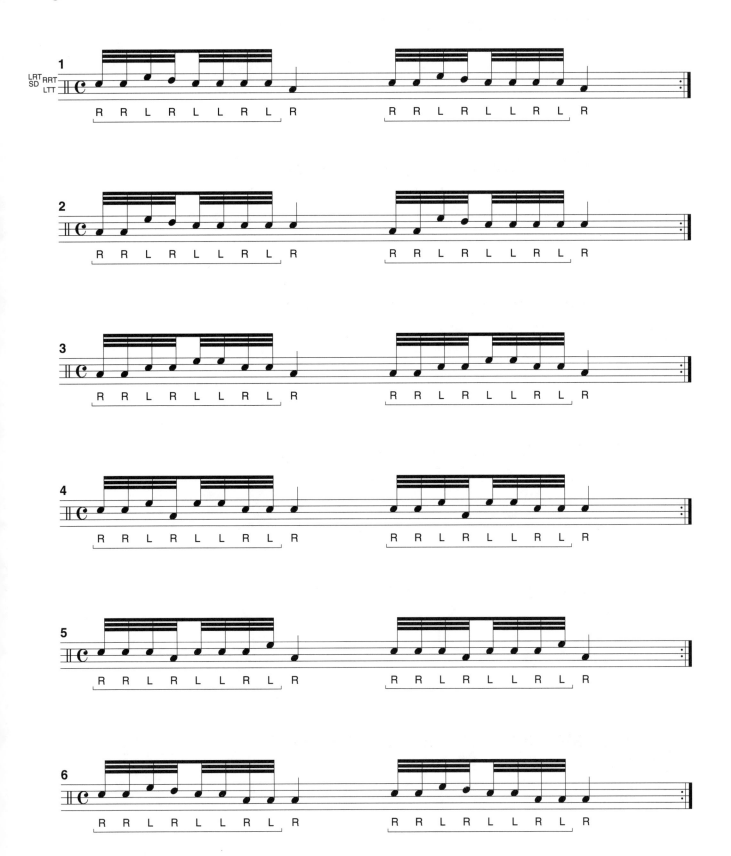

Two Groups Of 32nd Notes

Sticking: RLRLRLRL-RLRLRLRL-R

R L R L R L R L R L R L R L R L R

R L R L R L R L R L R L R L R L R

R L R L R L R L R L R L R L R L R

R L R L R L R L R L R L R L R L R

R L R L R L R L R L R L R L R L R

R L R L R L R L R L R L R L R L R

7

R L R L R L R L R L R L R L R L R

8

R L R L R L R L R L R L R L R L R

9

R L R L R L R L R L R L R L R L R

10

R L R L R L R L R L R L R L R L R

11

R L R L R L R L R L R L R L R L R

12

R L R L R L R L R L R L R L R L R

Sticking: RRLLRRLL-RRLLRRLL-R

R R L L R R L L R R L L R R L L R

R R L L R R L L R R L L R R L L R

R R L L R R L L R R L L R R L L R

R R L L R R L L R R L L R R L L R

R R L L R R L L R R L L R R L L R

R R L L R R L L R R L L R R L L R

Sticking: LLRRLLRR-LLRRLLRR-L

Sticking: RLRRLRLL-RLRRLRLL-R

Sticking: RRLRLLRL-RRLRLLRL-R

1

R R L R L L R L R R L R L L R L R

2

R R L R L L R L R R L R L L R L R

3

R R L R L L R L R R L R L L R L R

4

R R L R L L R L R R L R L L R L R

5

R R L R L L R L R R L R L L R L R

6

R R L R L L R L R R L R L L R L R

Three Groups Of 32nd Notes

Sticking: RLRLRLRL-RLRLRLRL-RLRLRLRL-R

Sticking: RRLLRRLL-RRLLRRLL-RRLLRRLL-R

1

R R L L R R L L R R L L R R L L R R L L R R L L R

2

R R L L R R L L R R L L R R L L R R L L R R L L R

3

R R L L R R L L R R L L R R L L R R L L R R L L R

4

R R L L R R L L R R L L R R L L R R L L R R L L R

5

R R L L R R L L R R L L R R L L R R L L R R L L R

6

R R L L R R L L R R L L R R L L R R L L R R L L R

Sticking: LLRRLLRR-LLRRLLRR-LLRRLLRR-L

1

LRT RRT
SD LTT

L L R R L L R R L L R R L L R R L L R R L L R R L

2

L L R R L L R R L L R R L L R R L L R R L L R R L

3

L L R R L L R R L L R R L L R R L L R R L L R R L

4

L L R R L L R R L L R R L L R R L L R R L L R R L

5

L L R R L L R R L L R R L L R R L L R R L L R R L

6

L L R R L L R R L L R R L L R R L L R R L L R R L

Sticking: RLRRLRLL-RLRRLRLL-RLRRLRLL-R

R L R R L R L L R L R R L R L L R L R R L R L L R

R L R R L R L L R L R R L R L L R L R R L R L L R

R L R R L R L L R L R R L R L L R L R R L R L L R

R L R R L R L L R L R R L R L L R L R R L R L L R

R L R R L R L L R L R R L R L L R L R R L R L L R

R L R R L R L L R L R R L R L L R L R R L R L L R

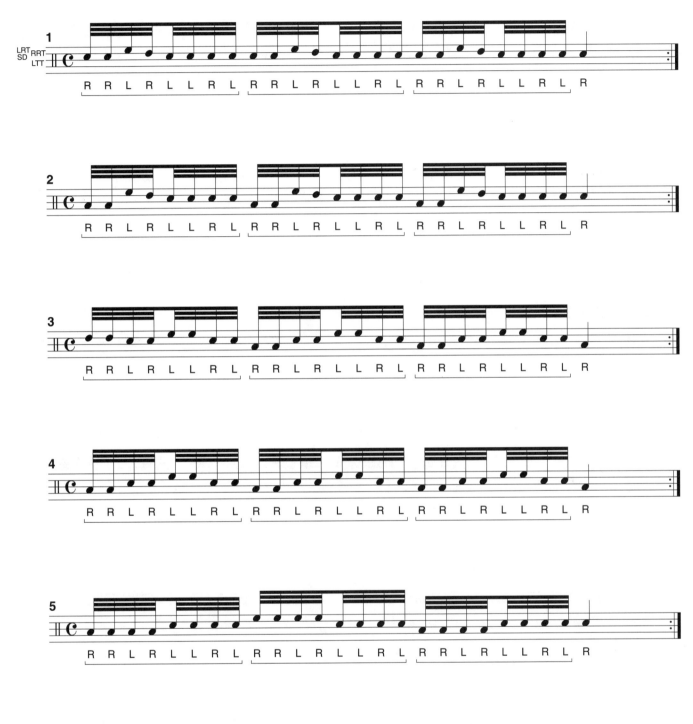

Four Groups Of 32nd Notes

Sticking: RLRLRLRL-RLRLRLRL-RLRLRLRL-RLRLRLRL

1

R L R L R L R L R L R L R L R L R L R L R L R L R L R L R L R L

2

R L R L R L R L R L R L R L R L R L R L R L R L R L R L R L R L

3

R L R L R L R L R L R L R L R L R L R L R L R L R L R L R L R L

4

R L R L R L R L R L R L R L R L R L R L R L R L R L R L R L R L

5

R L R L R L R L R L R L R L R L R L R L R L R L R L R L R L R L

6

R L R L R L R L R L R L R L R L R L R L R L R L R L R L R L R L

Sticking: RRLLRRLL-RRLLRRLL-RRLLRRLL-RRLLRRLL

72

Sticking: LLRRLLRR-LLRRLLRR-LLRRLLRR-LLRRLLRR

1

L L R R L L R R L L R R L L R R L L R R L L R R L L R R L L R R

2

L L R R L L R R L L R R L L R R L L R R L L R R L L R R L L R R

3

L L R R L L R R L L R R L L R R L L R R L L R R L L R R L L R R

4

L L R R L L R R L L R R L L R R L L R R L L R R L L R R L L R R

5

L L R R L L R R L L R R L L R R L L R R L L R R L L R R L L R R

6

L L R R L L R R L L R R L L R R L L R R L L R R L L R R L L R R

Sticking: RLRRLRLL-RLRRLRLL-RLRRLRLL-RLRRLRLL

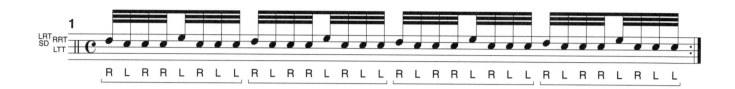

R L R R L R L L R L R R L R L L R L R R L R L L R L R R L R L L

R L R R L R L L R L R R L R L L R L R R L R L L R L R R L R L L

R L R R L R L L R L R R L R L L R L R R L R L L R L R R L R L L

R L R R L R L L R L R R L R L L R L R R L R L L R L R R L R L L

R L R R L R L L R L R R L R L L R L R R L R L L R L R R L R L L

R L R R L R L L R L R R L R L L R L R R L R L L R L R R L R L L

Sticking: RRLRLLRL-RRLRLLRL-RRLRLLRL-RRLRLLRL

1

R R L R L L R L R R L R L L R L R R L R L L R L R R L R L L R L

2

R R L R L L R L R R L R L L R L R R L R L L R L R R L R L L R L

3

R R L R L L R L R R L R L L R L R R L R L L R L R R L R L L R L

4

R R L R L L R L R R L R L L R L R R L R L L R L R R L R L L R L

5

R R L R L L R L R R L R L L R L R R L R L L R L R R L R L L R L

6

R R L R L L R L R R L R L L R L R R L R L L R L R R L R L L R L

Two-Bar Patterns

The ten two-bar 32nd-note patterns that follow require speed, control, and concentration. Practice them slowly at first and increase the tempo gradually. Be aware of the sticking change between the first and second bars.

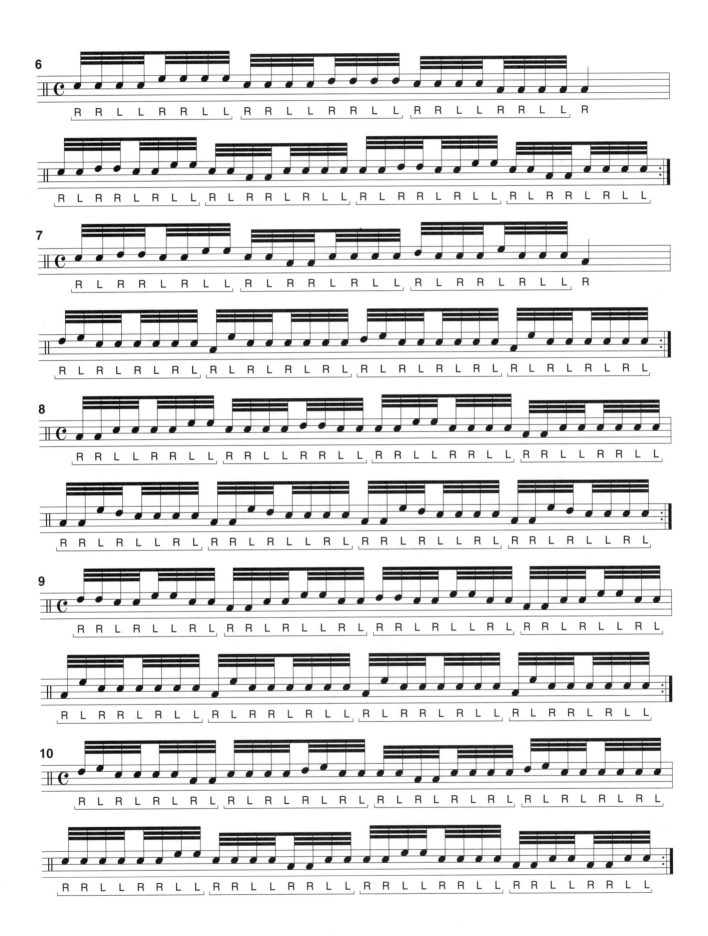

32nd-Note Fills

The fourth bar of each exercise below includes a 32nd-note fill. Each one is preceded by three bars of a 16th-note rock pattern using alternate sticking. The transition from the rock beat into the fill and back should flow smoothly and evenly. Practice these fills at varied tempos and dynamics.

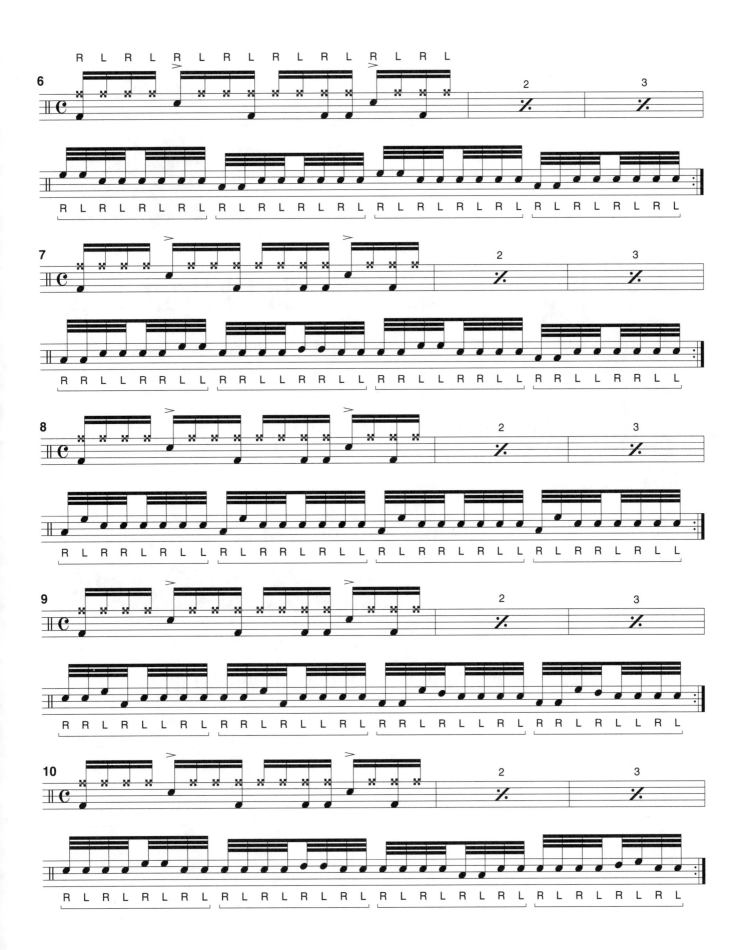